The Mind of a King
Goals Journal

THE MIND OF

_____
(Your Name Here)

GOD SAYS THAT YOU ARE...

NEVER ALONE	← • →	MATT 28:20
CHOSEN	← • →	I THESS 1:4
CAPABLE	← • →	MARK 10:27
AMAZING	← • →	PSALM 139:14
STRONG	← • →	PHIL 4:13
PROTECTED	← • →	PSALM 121:3
SPECIAL	← • →	EPHESIANS 2:10
VICTORIOUS	← • →	ROMAN 8:37

Because your mental health matters!

Countless studies have proven journaling to be immensely beneficial, to both our mental and physical health. It has been shown to enhance your memory and immune system, as well as improve your mood and battle stress/anxiety.

In order to be the best version of ourselves, for our families and/or our careers, we have to make time to take care of ourselves. This may look like waking up an hour (or a few) earlier than normal, to workout, have a cup of coffee, meditate, take a shower, read, clean your work area or anything that you can think of that will make the day run smoother for you. Taking the time to do something that brings you peace, will clear your mind and make you sharper, for the rest of the day.

Journaling can be a big part of that and it's one of the easiest ways to take better care of yourself. As a wife, a daughter, a sister, a mother and a bonus mother of kings and young kings, I desire to help encourage men to heal and express themselves. So my hope for this journal, is that it becomes a tool to help you take better care of yourself. get started early and make the time to enhance your skills, while staying on task.
Enjoy and be a greater you!

- Raichelle - designer/creator

LET'S GO! DATE: _____

▶ **GOALS**
- _____ ☐
- _____ ☐
- _____ ☐
- _____ ☐
- _____ ☐
- _____ ☐
- _____ ☐
- _____ ☐
- _____ ☐

▶ TODAY I STRUGGLED WITH...

_____
_____
_____
_____

▶ TODAY'S TOP ACHIEVEMENTS

▶ TODAY I FELT...

(CHOOSE ALL THAT APPLY)

▶ HOW WOULD YOU RATE THE DAY?
☆ ☆ ☆ ☆ ☆

▶ BUT I CAN CORRECT THAT BY...

_____
_____
_____
_____

▶ GYM GOALS
○ _____ ☐
○ _____ ☐
○ _____ ☐

▶ TODAY I'M GRATEFUL FOR...
○ _____
○ _____
○ _____

▶ NIGHT PREP FOR TOMORROW
○ _____
○ _____
○ _____

WHAT'S ON YOUR MIND

Use this space to write down **anything** on your mind, that may be influencing you; good, bad or indifferent.

_____

_____

_____

_____

_____

_____

_____

_____

_____

_____

_____

_____

_____

_____

_____

TOMORROW STARTS TODAY

LET'S GO! DATE: _____

▶ **G O A L S**

_____ ☐
_____ ☐
_____ ☐
_____ ☐
_____ ☐
_____ ☐
_____ ☐
_____ ☐

▶ TODAY I STRUGGLED WITH...

_____
_____
_____
_____

▶ BUT I CAN CORRECT THAT BY...

_____
_____
_____

▶ TODAY'S TOP ACHIEVEMENTS

▶ GYM GOALS
○ _____ ☐
○ _____ ☐
○ _____ ☐

▶ TODAY I'M GRATEFUL FOR...
○ _____
○ _____
○ _____

▶ TODAY I FELT...

(CHOOSE ALL THAT APPLY)

▶ NIGHT PREP FOR TOMORROW
○ _____
○ _____
○ _____

▶ HOW WOULD YOU RATE THE DAY?

☆ ☆ ☆ ☆ ☆

WHAT'S ON YOUR MIND

Use this space to write down **anything** on your mind, that may be influencing you;
good, bad or indifferent.

_____

_____

_____

_____

_____

_____

_____

_____

_____

_____

_____

_____

_____

_____

TOMORROW STARTS TODAY

LET'S GO! DATE: _____

▷ **GOALS**
_____ ☐
_____ ☐
_____ ☐
_____ ☐
_____ ☐
_____ ☐
_____ ☐
_____ ☐
_____ ☐

▷ TODAY I STRUGGLED WITH...
_____
_____
_____
_____

▷ BUT I CAN CORRECT THAT BY...
_____
_____
_____
_____

▷ TODAY'S TOP ACHIEVEMENTS

▷ GYM GOALS
○ _____ ☐
○ _____ ☐
○ _____ ☐

▷ TODAY I'M GRATEFUL FOR...
○ _____
○ _____
○ _____

▷ TODAY I FELT...

(CHOOSE ALL THAT APPLY)

▷ NIGHT PREP FOR TOMORROW
○ _____
○ _____
○ _____

▷ HOW WOULD YOU RATE THE DAY?
☆ ☆ ☆ ☆ ☆

WHAT'S ON YOUR MIND

Use this space to write down **anything** on your mind, that may be influencing you; good, bad or indifferent.

_____

_____

_____

_____

_____

_____

_____

_____

_____

_____

_____

_____

_____

_____

_____

_____

TOMORROW STARTS TODAY

LET'S GO! DATE: _____

▶ **GOALS**
_____ ☐
_____ ☐
_____ ☐
_____ ☐
_____ ☐
_____ ☐
_____ ☐
_____ ☐

▶ TODAY I STRUGGLED WITH...
_____
_____
_____
_____

▶ BUT I CAN CORRECT THAT BY...
_____
_____
_____
_____

▶ TODAY'S TOP ACHIEVEMENTS

▶ GYM GOALS
○ _____ ☐
○ _____ ☐
○ _____ ☐

▶ TODAY I'M GRATEFUL FOR...
○ _____
○ _____
○ _____

▶ TODAY I FELT...

(CHOOSE ALL THAT APPLY)

▶ NIGHT PREP FOR TOMORROW
○ _____
○ _____
○ _____

▶ HOW WOULD YOU RATE THE DAY?
☆ ☆ ☆ ☆ ☆

WHAT'S ON YOUR MIND

Use this space to write down **anything** on your mind, that may be influencing you; good, bad or indifferent.

_____

_____

_____

_____

_____

_____

_____

_____

_____

_____

_____

_____

_____

TOMORROW STARTS TODAY

LET'S GO! DATE: _____

▶ **GOALS**
- _____ ☑
- _____ ☐
- _____ ☐
- _____ ☐
- _____ ☐
- _____ ☐
- _____ ☐
- _____ ☐
- _____ ☐

▶ TODAY I STRUGGLED WITH...

_____
_____
_____
_____

▶ TODAY'S TOP ACHIEVEMENTS

▶ TODAY I FELT...

(CHOOSE ALL THAT APPLY)

▶ HOW WOULD YOU RATE THE DAY?
☆ ☆ ☆ ☆ ☆

▶ BUT I CAN CORRECT THAT BY...

_____
_____
_____
_____

▶ GYM GOALS
○ _____ ☐
○ _____ ☐
○ _____ ☐

▶ TODAY I'M GRATEFUL FOR...
○ _____
○ _____
○ _____

▶ NIGHT PREP FOR TOMORROW
○ _____
○ _____
○ _____

WHAT'S ON YOUR MIND

Use this space to write down **anything** on your mind, that may be influencing you; good, bad or indifferent.

_____

_____

_____

_____

_____

_____

_____

_____

_____

_____

_____

_____

_____

_____

_____

TOMORROW STARTS TODAY

LET'S GO! DATE: _____

▶ **GOALS**
- _____ ☐
- _____ ☐
- _____ ☐
- _____ ☐
- _____ ☐
- _____ ☐
- _____ ☐
- _____ ☐

▶ TODAY I STRUGGLED WITH...

_____
_____
_____
_____

▶ BUT I CAN CORRECT THAT BY...

_____
_____
_____
_____

▶ TODAY'S TOP ACHIEVEMENTS

▶ GYM GOALS
○ _____ ☐
○ _____ ☐
○ _____ ☐

▶ TODAY I'M GRATEFUL FOR...
○ _____
○ _____
○ _____

▶ TODAY I FELT...

(CHOOSE ALL THAT APPLY)

▶ NIGHT PREP FOR TOMORROW
○ _____
○ _____
○ _____

▶ HOW WOULD YOU RATE THE DAY?
☆ ☆ ☆ ☆ ☆

WHAT'S ON YOUR MIND

Use this space to write down **anything** on your mind, that may be influencing you; good, bad or indifferent.

_____

_____

_____

_____

_____

_____

_____

_____

_____

_____

_____

_____

_____

_____

TOMORROW STARTS TODAY

LET'S GO! DATE: _____

▷ **GOALS**
_____ ☐
_____ ☐
_____ ☐
_____ ☐
_____ ☐
_____ ☐
_____ ☐
_____ ☐
_____ ☐

▷ TODAY I STRUGGLED WITH...
_____
_____
_____
_____

▷ BUT I CAN CORRECT THAT BY...
_____
_____
_____

▷ TODAY'S TOP ACHIEVEMENTS

▷ GYM GOALS
○ _____ ☐
○ _____ ☐
○ _____ ☐

▷ TODAY I'M GRATEFUL FOR...
○ _____
○ _____
○ _____

▷ TODAY I FELT...

(CHOOSE ALL THAT APPLY)

▷ NIGHT PREP FOR TOMORROW
○ _____
○ _____
○ _____

▷ HOW WOULD YOU RATE THE DAY?
☆ ☆ ☆ ☆ ☆

WHAT'S ON YOUR MIND

Use this space to write down **anything** on your mind, that may be influencing you; good, bad or indifferent.

_____

_____

_____

_____

_____

_____

_____

_____

_____

_____

_____

_____

_____

_____

_____

_____

TOMORROW STARTS TODAY

LET'S GO! DATE: _____

▶ **GOALS**
_____ ☐
_____ ☐
_____ ☐
_____ ☐
_____ ☐
_____ ☐
_____ ☐
_____ ☐

▶ TODAY I STRUGGLED WITH...
_____
_____
_____
_____

▶ BUT I CAN CORRECT THAT BY...
_____
_____
_____

▶ TODAY'S TOP ACHIEVEMENTS

▶ GYM GOALS
○ _____ ☐
○ _____ ☐
○ _____ ☐

▶ TODAY I'M GRATEFUL FOR...
○ _____
○ _____
○ _____

▶ TODAY I FELT...

(CHOOSE ALL THAT APPLY)

▶ NIGHT PREP FOR TOMORROW
○ _____
○ _____
○ _____

▶ HOW WOULD YOU RATE THE DAY?
☆ ☆ ☆ ☆ ☆

WHAT'S ON YOUR MIND

Use this space to write down **anything** on your mind, that may be influencing you; good, bad or indifferent.

_____

_____

_____

_____

_____

_____

_____

_____

_____

_____

_____

_____

_____

_____

_____

_____

TOMORROW STARTS TODAY

LET'S GO! DATE: _____

▷ G _____ ☐
   O _____ ☐
   A _____ ☐
   L _____ ☐
   S _____ ☐
   _____ ☐
   _____ ☐
   _____ ☐
   _____ ☐

▷ TODAY I STRUGGLED WITH...   ▷ BUT I CAN CORRECT THAT BY...
_____   _____
_____   _____
_____   _____
_____

                                    ▷ GYM GOALS
▷ TODAY'S TOP ACHIEVEMENTS   ○ _____ ☐
                                    ○ _____ ☐
                                    ○ _____ ☐

                                    ▷ TODAY I'M GRATEFUL FOR...
                                    ○ _____
                                    ○ _____
                                    ○ _____

▷ TODAY I FELT...
☺ 😐 😖 😟 😠 ☹

(CHOOSE ALL THAT APPLY)   ▷ NIGHT PREP FOR TOMORROW
                                    ○ _____
▷ HOW WOULD YOU RATE THE DAY?   ○ _____
☆ ☆ ☆ ☆ ☆   ○ _____

WHAT'S ON YOUR MIND

Use this space to write down **anything** on your mind, that may be influencing you; good, bad or indifferent.

_____

_____

_____

_____

_____

_____

_____

_____

_____

_____

_____

_____

_____

_____

_____

TOMORROW STARTS TODAY

LET'S GO! DATE: _____

▶ **GOALS**

- _____ ☐
- _____ ☐
- _____ ☐
- _____ ☐
- _____ ☐
- _____ ☐
- _____ ☐
- _____ ☐

▶ TODAY I STRUGGLED WITH...

_____
_____
_____
_____

▶ BUT I CAN CORRECT THAT BY...

_____
_____
_____

▶ TODAY'S TOP ACHIEVEMENTS

▶ **GYM GOALS**
- ○ _____ ☐
- ○ _____ ☐
- ○ _____ ☐

▶ TODAY I'M GRATEFUL FOR...
- ○ _____
- ○ _____
- ○ _____

▶ TODAY I FELT...

(CHOOSE ALL THAT APPLY)

▶ NIGHT PREP FOR TOMORROW
- ○ _____
- ○ _____
- ○ _____

▶ HOW WOULD YOU RATE THE DAY?

☆ ☆ ☆ ☆ ☆

WHAT'S ON YOUR MIND

Use this space to write down **anything** on your mind, that may be influencing you; good, bad or indifferent.

TOMORROW STARTS TODAY

LET'S GO! DATE: _____

▶ **G O A L S**

- _____ ☐
- _____ ☐
- _____ ☐
- _____ ☐
- _____ ☐
- _____ ☐
- _____ ☐
- _____ ☐

▶ TODAY I STRUGGLED WITH...

_____
_____
_____
_____

▶ BUT I CAN CORRECT THAT BY...

_____
_____
_____

▶ TODAY'S TOP ACHIEVEMENTS

▶ GYM GOALS

○ _____ ☐
○ _____ ☐
○ _____ ☐

▶ TODAY I'M GRATEFUL FOR...

○ _____
○ _____
○ _____

▶ TODAY I FELT...

(CHOOSE ALL THAT APPLY)

▶ NIGHT PREP FOR TOMORROW

○ _____
○ _____
○ _____

▶ HOW WOULD YOU RATE THE DAY?

☆ ☆ ☆ ☆ ☆

WHAT'S ON YOUR MIND

Use this space to write down **anything** on your mind, that may be influencing you; good, bad or indifferent.

_____

_____

_____

_____

_____

_____

_____

_____

_____

_____

_____

_____

_____

_____

_____

TOMORROW STARTS TODAY

LET'S GO! DATE: _____

▷ **GOALS**
_____ ☐
_____ ☐
_____ ☐
_____ ☐
_____ ☐
_____ ☐
_____ ☐
_____ ☐
_____ ☐

▷ TODAY I STRUGGLED WITH...
_____
_____
_____
_____

▷ BUT I CAN CORRECT THAT BY...
_____
_____
_____

▷ TODAY'S TOP ACHIEVEMENTS

▷ GYM GOALS
○ _____ ☐
○ _____ ☐
○ _____ ☐

▷ TODAY I'M GRATEFUL FOR...
○ _____
○ _____
○ _____

▷ TODAY I FELT...

(CHOOSE ALL THAT APPLY)

▷ NIGHT PREP FOR TOMORROW
○ _____
○ _____
○ _____

▷ HOW WOULD YOU RATE THE DAY?
☆ ☆ ☆ ☆ ☆

WHAT'S ON YOUR MIND

Use this space to write down **anything** on your mind, that may be influencing you; good, bad or indifferent.

TOMORROW STARTS TODAY

LET'S GO! DATE: _____

▷ **GOALS**
- ☐ _____
- ☐ _____
- ☐ _____
- ☐ _____
- ☐ _____
- ☐ _____
- ☐ _____
- ☐ _____

▷ TODAY I STRUGGLED WITH...

_____
_____
_____
_____

▷ BUT I CAN CORRECT THAT BY...

_____
_____
_____
_____

▷ TODAY'S TOP ACHIEVEMENTS

▷ GYM GOALS
- ○ _____ ☐
- ○ _____ ☐
- ○ _____ ☐

▷ TODAY I'M GRATEFUL FOR...
- ○ _____
- ○ _____
- ○ _____

▷ TODAY I FELT...

(CHOOSE ALL THAT APPLY)

▷ NIGHT PREP FOR TOMORROW
- ○ _____
- ○ _____
- ○ _____

▷ HOW WOULD YOU RATE THE DAY?

☆ ☆ ☆ ☆ ☆

WHAT'S ON YOUR MIND

Use this space to write down **anything** on your mind, that may be influencing you; good, bad or indifferent.

TOMORROW STARTS TODAY

LET'S GO! DATE: _____

GOALS

☑
☐
☐
☐
☐
☐
☐
☐
☐

▶ TODAY I STRUGGLED WITH...

_____
_____
_____
_____

▶ BUT I CAN CORRECT THAT BY...

_____
_____
_____

▶ TODAY'S TOP ACHIEVEMENTS

▶ GYM GOALS
○ _____ ☐
○ _____ ☐
○ _____ ☐

▶ TODAY I'M GRATEFUL FOR...
○ _____
○ _____
○ _____

▶ TODAY I FELT...

(CHOOSE ALL THAT APPLY)

▶ NIGHT PREP FOR TOMORROW
○ _____
○ _____
○ _____

▶ HOW WOULD YOU RATE THE DAY?
☆ ☆ ☆ ☆ ☆

WHAT'S ON YOUR MIND

Use this space to write down **anything** on your mind, that may be influencing you; good, bad or indifferent.

_____

_____

_____

_____

_____

_____

_____

_____

_____

_____

_____

_____

_____

_____

TOMORROW STARTS TODAY

LET'S GO! DATE: _____

▶ GOALS

- ☐
- ☐
- ☐
- ☐
- ☐
- ☐
- ☐
- ☐

▶ TODAY I STRUGGLED WITH...

_____
_____
_____
_____

▶ BUT I CAN CORRECT THAT BY...

_____
_____
_____

▶ TODAY'S TOP ACHIEVEMENTS

▶ GYM GOALS
- ○ _____ ☐
- ○ _____ ☐
- ○ _____ ☐

▶ TODAY I'M GRATEFUL FOR...
- ○ _____
- ○ _____
- ○ _____

▶ TODAY I FELT...

(CHOOSE ALL THAT APPLY)

▶ NIGHT PREP FOR TOMORROW
- ○ _____
- ○ _____
- ○ _____

▶ HOW WOULD YOU RATE THE DAY?

☆ ☆ ☆ ☆ ☆

WHAT'S ON YOUR MIND

Use this space to write down **anything** on your mind, that may be influencing you;
good, bad or indifferent.

_____

_____

_____

_____

_____

_____

_____

_____

_____

_____

_____

_____

_____

TOMORROW STARTS TODAY

LET'S GO! DATE: _____

▶ G
O
A
L
S
_____ ☐
_____ ☐
_____ ☐
_____ ☐
_____ ☐
_____ ☐
_____ ☐
_____ ☐
_____ ☐

▶ TODAY I STRUGGLED WITH...

_____
_____
_____
_____

▶ BUT I CAN CORRECT THAT BY...

_____
_____
_____

▶ TODAY'S TOP ACHIEVEMENTS

▶ GYM GOALS
○ _____ ☐
○ _____ ☐
○ _____ ☐

▶ TODAY I'M GRATEFUL FOR...
○ _____
○ _____
○ _____

▶ TODAY I FELT...

(CHOOSE ALL THAT APPLY)

▶ NIGHT PREP FOR TOMORROW
○ _____
○ _____
○ _____

▶ HOW WOULD YOU RATE THE DAY?
☆ ☆ ☆ ☆ ☆

WHAT'S ON YOUR MIND

Use this space to write down **anything** on your mind, that may be influencing you; good, bad or indifferent.

_____

_____

_____

_____

_____

_____

_____

_____

_____

_____

_____

_____

_____

_____

_____

_____

TOMORROW STARTS TODAY

LET'S GO! DATE: _____

GOALS

▷
- _____ ☐
- _____ ☐
- _____ ☐
- _____ ☐
- _____ ☐
- _____ ☐
- _____ ☐
- _____ ☐
- _____ ☐

▷ **TODAY I STRUGGLED WITH...**

_____
_____
_____
_____

▷ **BUT I CAN CORRECT THAT BY...**

_____
_____
_____

▷ **TODAY'S TOP ACHIEVEMENTS**

▷ **GYM GOALS**
- ○ _____ ☐
- ○ _____ ☐
- ○ _____ ☐

▷ **TODAY I'M GRATEFUL FOR...**
- ○ _____
- ○ _____
- ○ _____

▷ **TODAY I FELT...**

(CHOOSE ALL THAT APPLY)

▷ **HOW WOULD YOU RATE THE DAY?**

☆ ☆ ☆ ☆ ☆

▷ **NIGHT PREP FOR TOMORROW**
- ○ _____
- ○ _____
- ○ _____

WHAT'S ON YOUR MIND

Use this space to write down **anything** on your mind, that may be influencing you; good, bad or indifferent.

_____

_____

_____

_____

_____

_____

_____

_____

_____

_____

_____

_____

_____

_____

TOMORROW STARTS TODAY

LET'S GO! DATE: _____

▶ **G O A L S**
- _____ ☐
- _____ ☐
- _____ ☐
- _____ ☐
- _____ ☐
- _____ ☐
- _____ ☐
- _____ ☐

▶ TODAY I STRUGGLED WITH...
_____
_____
_____
_____

▶ TODAY'S TOP ACHIEVEMENTS

▶ TODAY I FELT...

(CHOOSE ALL THAT APPLY)

▶ HOW WOULD YOU RATE THE DAY?
☆ ☆ ☆ ☆ ☆

▶ BUT I CAN CORRECT THAT BY...
_____
_____
_____

▶ GYM GOALS
○ _____ ☐
○ _____ ☐
○ _____ ☐

▶ TODAY I'M GRATEFUL FOR...
○ _____
○ _____
○ _____

▶ NIGHT PREP FOR TOMORROW
○ _____
○ _____
○ _____

WHAT'S ON YOUR MIND

Use this space to write down **anything** on your mind, that may be influencing you; good, bad or indifferent.

_____

_____

_____

_____

_____

_____

_____

_____

_____

_____

_____

_____

_____

_____

_____

_____

TOMORROW STARTS TODAY

LET'S GO! DATE: _____

▶ **GOALS**
- _____ ☐
- _____ ☐
- _____ ☐
- _____ ☐
- _____ ☐
- _____ ☐
- _____ ☐
- _____ ☐

▶ TODAY I STRUGGLED WITH...

_____
_____
_____
_____

▶ BUT I CAN CORRECT THAT BY...

_____
_____
_____

▶ TODAY'S TOP ACHIEVEMENTS

▶ GYM GOALS
- ○ _____ ☐
- ○ _____ ☐
- ○ _____ ☐

▶ TODAY I'M GRATEFUL FOR...
- ○ _____
- ○ _____
- ○ _____

▶ TODAY I FELT...

(CHOOSE ALL THAT APPLY)

▶ HOW WOULD YOU RATE THE DAY?

☆ ☆ ☆ ☆ ☆

▶ NIGHT PREP FOR TOMORROW
- ○ _____
- ○ _____
- ○ _____

WHAT'S ON YOUR MIND

Use this space to write down **anything** on your mind, that may be influencing you; good, bad or indifferent.

_____

_____

_____

_____

_____

_____

_____

_____

_____

_____

_____

_____

_____

_____

_____

_____

TOMORROW STARTS TODAY

LET'S GO! DATE: _____

GOALS

☐ _____
☐ _____
☐ _____
☐ _____
☐ _____
☐ _____
☐ _____
☐ _____
☐ _____

▶ **TODAY I STRUGGLED WITH...**

_____
_____
_____
_____

▶ **TODAY'S TOP ACHIEVEMENTS**

▶ **TODAY I FELT...**

(CHOOSE ALL THAT APPLY)

▶ **HOW WOULD YOU RATE THE DAY?**

☆ ☆ ☆ ☆ ☆

▶ **BUT I CAN CORRECT THAT BY...**

_____
_____
_____
_____

▶ **GYM GOALS**

○ _____ ☐
○ _____ ☐
○ _____ ☐

▶ **TODAY I'M GRATEFUL FOR...**

○ _____
○ _____
○ _____

▶ **NIGHT PREP FOR TOMORROW**

○ _____
○ _____
○ _____

WHAT'S ON YOUR MIND

Use this space to write down **anything** on your mind, that may be influencing you; good, bad or indifferent.

TOMORROW STARTS TODAY

LET'S GO! DATE: _____

▶ **GOALS**

☐
☐
☐
☐
☐
☐
☐
☐

▶ TODAY I STRUGGLED WITH...

_____
_____
_____
_____

▶ BUT I CAN CORRECT THAT BY...

_____
_____
_____

▶ GYM GOALS
○ _____ ☐
○ _____ ☐
○ _____ ☐

▶ TODAY'S TOP ACHIEVEMENTS

▶ TODAY I'M GRATEFUL FOR...
○ _____
○ _____
○ _____

▶ TODAY I FELT...

(CHOOSE ALL THAT APPLY)

▶ NIGHT PREP FOR TOMORROW
○ _____
○ _____
○ _____

▶ HOW WOULD YOU RATE THE DAY?
☆ ☆ ☆ ☆ ☆

WHAT'S ON YOUR MIND

Use this space to write down **anything** on your mind, that may be influencing you;
good, bad or indifferent.

_____

_____

_____

_____

_____

_____

_____

_____

_____

_____

_____

_____

_____

_____

TOMORROW STARTS TODAY

LET'S GO! DATE: _____

▶ **GOALS**

☑ _____
☐ _____
☐ _____
☐ _____
☐ _____
☐ _____
☐ _____
☐ _____

▶ TODAY I STRUGGLED WITH...

_____
_____
_____
_____

▶ TODAY'S TOP ACHIEVEMENTS

▶ TODAY I FELT...

(CHOOSE ALL THAT APPLY)

▶ HOW WOULD YOU RATE THE DAY?

☆ ☆ ☆ ☆ ☆

▶ BUT I CAN CORRECT THAT BY...

_____
_____
_____

▶ GYM GOALS
○ _____ ☐
○ _____ ☐
○ _____ ☐

▶ TODAY I'M GRATEFUL FOR...
○ _____
○ _____
○ _____

▶ NIGHT PREP FOR TOMORROW
○ _____
○ _____
○ _____

WHAT'S ON YOUR MIND

Use this space to write down **anything** on your mind, that may be influencing you; good, bad or indifferent.

TOMORROW STARTS TODAY

LET'S GO! DATE: _____

▶ **GOALS**
_____ ☐
_____ ☐
_____ ☐
_____ ☐
_____ ☐
_____ ☐
_____ ☐
_____ ☐

▶ TODAY I STRUGGLED WITH...
_____
_____
_____
_____

▶ BUT I CAN CORRECT THAT BY...
_____
_____
_____

▶ TODAY'S TOP ACHIEVEMENTS

▶ GYM GOALS
○ _____ ☐
○ _____ ☐
○ _____ ☐

▶ TODAY I'M GRATEFUL FOR...
○ _____
○ _____
○ _____

▶ TODAY I FELT...
(CHOOSE ALL THAT APPLY)

▶ HOW WOULD YOU RATE THE DAY?
☆ ☆ ☆ ☆ ☆

▶ NIGHT PREP FOR TOMORROW
○ _____
○ _____
○ _____

WHAT'S ON YOUR MIND

Use this space to write down **anything** on your mind, that may be influencing you; good, bad or indifferent.

_____

_____

_____

_____

_____

_____

_____

_____

_____

_____

_____

_____

_____

_____

TOMORROW STARTS TODAY

LET'S GO! DATE: _____

▶ **GOALS**
_____ ☐
_____ ☐
_____ ☐
_____ ☐
_____ ☐
_____ ☐
_____ ☐
_____ ☐
_____ ☐

▶ TODAY I STRUGGLED WITH...

_____
_____
_____
_____

▶ TODAY'S TOP ACHIEVEMENTS

▶ TODAY I FELT...

(CHOOSE ALL THAT APPLY)

▶ HOW WOULD YOU RATE THE DAY?

☆ ☆ ☆ ☆ ☆

▶ BUT I CAN CORRECT THAT BY...

_____
_____
_____

▶ GYM GOALS
○ _____ ☐
○ _____ ☐
○ _____ ☐

▶ TODAY I'M GRATEFUL FOR...
○ _____
○ _____
○ _____

▶ NIGHT PREP FOR TOMORROW
○ _____
○ _____
○ _____

WHAT'S ON YOUR MIND

Use this space to write down **anything** on your mind, that may be influencing you; good, bad or indifferent.

_____

_____

_____

_____

_____

_____

_____

_____

_____

_____

_____

_____

_____

_____

_____

_____

TOMORROW STARTS TODAY

LET'S GO! DATE: _____

▶ GOALS
_____ ☐
_____ ☐
_____ ☐
_____ ☐
_____ ☐
_____ ☐
_____ ☐
_____ ☐
_____ ☐

▶ TODAY I STRUGGLED WITH...
_____
_____
_____
_____

▶ BUT I CAN CORRECT THAT BY...
_____
_____
_____

▶ TODAY'S TOP ACHIEVEMENTS

▶ GYM GOALS
○ _____ ☐
○ _____ ☐
○ _____ ☐

▶ TODAY I'M GRATEFUL FOR...
○ _____
○ _____
○ _____

▶ TODAY I FELT...
(CHOOSE ALL THAT APPLY)

▶ NIGHT PREP FOR TOMORROW
○ _____
○ _____
○ _____

▶ HOW WOULD YOU RATE THE DAY?
☆ ☆ ☆ ☆ ☆

WHAT'S ON YOUR MIND

Use this space to write down **anything** on your mind, that may be influencing you; good, bad or indifferent.

_____

_____

_____

_____

_____

_____

_____

_____

_____

_____

_____

_____

_____

_____

_____

_____

_____

TOMORROW STARTS TODAY

LET'S GO! DATE: _____

GOALS

- ☑ _____
- ☐ _____
- ☐ _____
- ☐ _____
- ☐ _____
- ☐ _____
- ☐ _____
- ☐ _____
- ☐ _____

▶ **TODAY I STRUGGLED WITH...**

_____
_____
_____
_____

▶ **TODAY'S TOP ACHIEVEMENTS**

▶ **TODAY I FELT...**

😊 😐 😖 😌 😠 ☹️

(CHOOSE ALL THAT APPLY)

▶ **HOW WOULD YOU RATE THE DAY?**

☆ ☆ ☆ ☆ ☆

▶ **BUT I CAN CORRECT THAT BY...**

_____
_____
_____

▶ **GYM GOALS**
- ○ _____ ☐
- ○ _____ ☐
- ○ _____ ☐

▶ **TODAY I'M GRATEFUL FOR...**
- ○ _____
- ○ _____
- ○ _____

▶ **NIGHT PREP FOR TOMORROW**
- ○ _____
- ○ _____
- ○ _____

WHAT'S ON YOUR MIND

Use this space to write down **anything** on your mind, that may be influencing you; good, bad or indifferent.

_____

_____

_____

_____

_____

_____

_____

_____

_____

_____

_____

_____

_____

_____

_____

_____

_____

TOMORROW STARTS TODAY

LET'S GO! DATE: _____

▶ **GOALS**

- _____ ☐
- _____ ☐
- _____ ☐
- _____ ☐
- _____ ☐
- _____ ☐
- _____ ☐
- _____ ☐

▶ TODAY I STRUGGLED WITH...

_____
_____
_____
_____

▶ BUT I CAN CORRECT THAT BY...

_____
_____
_____

▶ TODAY'S TOP ACHIEVEMENTS

▶ GYM GOALS
○ _____ ☐
○ _____ ☐
○ _____ ☐

▶ TODAY I'M GRATEFUL FOR...
○ _____
○ _____
○ _____

▶ TODAY I FELT...

(CHOOSE ALL THAT APPLY)

▶ NIGHT PREP FOR TOMORROW
○ _____
○ _____
○ _____

▶ HOW WOULD YOU RATE THE DAY?

☆ ☆ ☆ ☆ ☆

WHAT'S ON YOUR MIND

Use this space to write down **anything** on your mind, that may be influencing you; good, bad or indifferent.

_____

_____

_____

_____

_____

_____

_____

_____

_____

_____

_____

_____

_____

_____

_____

TOMORROW STARTS TODAY

LET'S GO! DATE: _____

▶ **GOALS**
_____ ☐
_____ ☐
_____ ☐
_____ ☐
_____ ☐
_____ ☐
_____ ☐
_____ ☐

▶ TODAY I STRUGGLED WITH...
_____
_____
_____
_____

▶ BUT I CAN CORRECT THAT BY...
_____
_____
_____

▶ TODAY'S TOP ACHIEVEMENTS

▶ GYM GOALS
○ _____ ☐
○ _____ ☐
○ _____ ☐

▶ TODAY I'M GRATEFUL FOR...
○ _____
○ _____
○ _____

▶ TODAY I FELT...
(CHOOSE ALL THAT APPLY)

▶ NIGHT PREP FOR TOMORROW
○ _____
○ _____
○ _____

▶ HOW WOULD YOU RATE THE DAY?
☆ ☆ ☆ ☆ ☆

WHAT'S ON YOUR MIND

Use this space to write down **anything** on your mind, that may be influencing you; good, bad or indifferent.

_____

_____

_____

_____

_____

_____

_____

_____

_____

_____

_____

_____

_____

_____

_____

TOMORROW STARTS TODAY

LET'S GO! DATE: _____

▶ GOALS

_____ ☐
_____ ☐
_____ ☐
_____ ☐
_____ ☐
_____ ☐
_____ ☐
_____ ☐

▶ TODAY I STRUGGLED WITH...

_____
_____
_____
_____

▶ TODAY'S TOP ACHIEVEMENTS

▶ TODAY I FELT...

(CHOOSE ALL THAT APPLY)

▶ HOW WOULD YOU RATE THE DAY?
☆ ☆ ☆ ☆ ☆

▶ BUT I CAN CORRECT THAT BY...

_____
_____
_____
_____

▶ GYM GOALS
○ _____ ☐
○ _____ ☐
○ _____ ☐

▶ TODAY I'M GRATEFUL FOR...
○ _____
○ _____
○ _____

▶ NIGHT PREP FOR TOMORROW
○ _____
○ _____
○ _____

WHAT'S ON YOUR MIND

Use this space to write down **anything** on your mind, that may be influencing you; good, bad or indifferent.

_____

_____

_____

_____

_____

_____

_____

_____

_____

_____

_____

_____

_____

_____

TOMORROW STARTS TODAY

LET'S GO! DATE: _____

GOALS

▶ _____ ☐
_____ ☐
_____ ☐
_____ ☐
_____ ☐
_____ ☐
_____ ☐
_____ ☐

▶ **TODAY I STRUGGLED WITH...**

_____
_____
_____
_____

▶ **TODAY'S TOP ACHIEVEMENTS**

▶ **TODAY I FELT...**

(CHOOSE ALL THAT APPLY)

▶ **HOW WOULD YOU RATE THE DAY?**

☆ ☆ ☆ ☆ ☆

▶ **BUT I CAN CORRECT THAT BY...**

_____
_____
_____

▶ **GYM GOALS**
○ _____ ☐
○ _____ ☐
○ _____ ☐

▶ **TODAY I'M GRATEFUL FOR...**
○ _____
○ _____
○ _____

▶ **NIGHT PREP FOR TOMORROW**
○ _____
○ _____
○ _____

WHAT'S ON YOUR MIND

Use this space to write down **anything** on your mind, that may be influencing you; good, bad or indifferent.

TOMORROW STARTS TODAY

LET'S GO! DATE: _____

▶ **GOALS**
- _____ ☐
- _____ ☐
- _____ ☐
- _____ ☐
- _____ ☐
- _____ ☐
- _____ ☐
- _____ ☐

▶ **TODAY I STRUGGLED WITH...**
_____
_____
_____
_____

▶ **BUT I CAN CORRECT THAT BY...**
_____
_____
_____

▶ **TODAY'S TOP ACHIEVEMENTS**

▶ **GYM GOALS**
○ _____ ☐
○ _____ ☐
○ _____ ☐

▶ **TODAY I'M GRATEFUL FOR...**
○ _____
○ _____
○ _____

▶ **TODAY I FELT...**

(CHOOSE ALL THAT APPLY)

▶ **NIGHT PREP FOR TOMORROW**
○ _____
○ _____
○ _____

▶ **HOW WOULD YOU RATE THE DAY?**
☆ ☆ ☆ ☆ ☆

WHAT'S ON YOUR MIND

Use this space to write down **anything** on your mind, that may be influencing you; good, bad or indifferent.

_____

_____

_____

_____

_____

_____

_____

_____

_____

_____

_____

_____

_____

_____

_____

TOMORROW STARTS TODAY

LET'S GO! DATE: _____

▶ GOALS

- _____ ☐
- _____ ☐
- _____ ☐
- _____ ☐
- _____ ☐
- _____ ☐
- _____ ☐
- _____ ☐
- _____ ☐

▶ TODAY I STRUGGLED WITH...

_____
_____
_____
_____

▶ BUT I CAN CORRECT THAT BY...

_____
_____
_____

▶ TODAY'S TOP ACHIEVEMENTS

▶ GYM GOALS
- ○ _____ ☐
- ○ _____ ☐
- ○ _____ ☐

▶ TODAY I'M GRATEFUL FOR...
- ○ _____
- ○ _____
- ○ _____

▶ TODAY I FELT...

(CHOOSE ALL THAT APPLY)

▶ NIGHT PREP FOR TOMORROW
- ○ _____
- ○ _____
- ○ _____

▶ HOW WOULD YOU RATE THE DAY?

☆ ☆ ☆ ☆ ☆

WHAT'S ON YOUR MIND

Use this space to write down **anything** on your mind, that may be influencing you; good, bad or indifferent.

_____

_____

_____

_____

_____

_____

_____

_____

_____

_____

_____

_____

_____

_____

_____

_____

TOMORROW STARTS TODAY

LET'S GO! DATE: _____

▶ **GOALS**
- _____ ☐
- _____ ☐
- _____ ☐
- _____ ☐
- _____ ☐
- _____ ☐
- _____ ☐
- _____ ☐

▶ TODAY I STRUGGLED WITH...
_____
_____
_____
_____

▶ BUT I CAN CORRECT THAT BY...
_____
_____
_____

▶ TODAY'S TOP ACHIEVEMENTS

▶ GYM GOALS
- ○ _____ ☐
- ○ _____ ☐
- ○ _____ ☐

▶ TODAY I'M GRATEFUL FOR...
- ○ _____
- ○ _____
- ○ _____

▶ TODAY I FELT...
(CHOOSE ALL THAT APPLY)

▶ NIGHT PREP FOR TOMORROW
- ○ _____
- ○ _____
- ○ _____

▶ HOW WOULD YOU RATE THE DAY?
☆ ☆ ☆ ☆ ☆

WHAT'S ON YOUR MIND

Use this space to write down **anything** on your mind, that may be influencing you; good, bad or indifferent.

_____

_____

_____

_____

_____

_____

_____

_____

_____

_____

_____

_____

_____

_____

_____

TOMORROW STARTS TODAY

LET'S GO! DATE: _____

▶ **G O A L S**
- _____ ☐
- _____ ☐
- _____ ☐
- _____ ☐
- _____ ☐
- _____ ☐
- _____ ☐
- _____ ☐

▶ TODAY I STRUGGLED WITH...
_____
_____
_____
_____

▶ BUT I CAN CORRECT THAT BY...
_____
_____
_____

▶ TODAY'S TOP ACHIEVEMENTS

▶ GYM GOALS
- ○ _____ ☐
- ○ _____ ☐
- ○ _____ ☐

▶ TODAY I'M GRATEFUL FOR...
- ○ _____
- ○ _____
- ○ _____

▶ TODAY I FELT...

(CHOOSE ALL THAT APPLY)

▶ NIGHT PREP FOR TOMORROW
- ○ _____
- ○ _____
- ○ _____

▶ HOW WOULD YOU RATE THE DAY?
☆ ☆ ☆ ☆ ☆

WHAT'S ON YOUR MIND

Use this space to write down **anything** on your mind, that may be influencing you; good, bad or indifferent.

TOMORROW STARTS TODAY

LET'S GO! DATE: _____

▶ **GOALS**

- ☐
- ☐
- ☐
- ☐
- ☐
- ☐
- ☐
- ☐

▶ TODAY I STRUGGLED WITH...

_____
_____
_____
_____

▶ BUT I CAN CORRECT THAT BY...

_____
_____
_____

▶ TODAY'S TOP ACHIEVEMENTS

▶ GYM GOALS
- ○ _____ ☐
- ○ _____ ☐
- ○ _____ ☐

▶ TODAY I'M GRATEFUL FOR...
- ○ _____
- ○ _____
- ○ _____

▶ TODAY I FELT...

(CHOOSE ALL THAT APPLY)

▶ HOW WOULD YOU RATE THE DAY?

☆ ☆ ☆ ☆ ☆

▶ NIGHT PREP FOR TOMORROW
- ○ _____
- ○ _____
- ○ _____

WHAT'S ON YOUR MIND

Use this space to write down **anything** on your mind, that may be influencing you; good, bad or indifferent.

_____

_____

_____

_____

_____

_____

_____

_____

_____

_____

_____

_____

_____

_____

_____

TOMORROW STARTS TODAY

LET'S GO! DATE: _____

GOALS

▶ GOALS
- _____ ☐
- _____ ☐
- _____ ☐
- _____ ☐
- _____ ☐
- _____ ☐
- _____ ☐
- _____ ☐
- _____ ☐

▶ TODAY I STRUGGLED WITH...

_____
_____
_____
_____

▶ BUT I CAN CORRECT THAT BY...

_____
_____
_____

▶ TODAY'S TOP ACHIEVEMENTS

▶ GYM GOALS
- ○ _____ ☐
- ○ _____ ☐
- ○ _____ ☐

▶ TODAY I'M GRATEFUL FOR...
- ○ _____
- ○ _____
- ○ _____

▶ TODAY I FELT...

(CHOOSE ALL THAT APPLY)

▶ NIGHT PREP FOR TOMORROW
- ○ _____
- ○ _____
- ○ _____

▶ HOW WOULD YOU RATE THE DAY?

☆ ☆ ☆ ☆ ☆

WHAT'S ON YOUR MIND

Use this space to write down **anything** on your mind, that may be influencing you; good, bad or indifferent.

_____

_____

_____

_____

_____

_____

_____

_____

_____

_____

_____

_____

_____

_____

_____

TOMORROW STARTS TODAY

LET'S GO! DATE: _____

▶ **GOALS**
- _____ ☐
- _____ ☐
- _____ ☐
- _____ ☐
- _____ ☐
- _____ ☐
- _____ ☐
- _____ ☐
- _____ ☐

▶ TODAY I STRUGGLED WITH...

_____
_____
_____
_____

▶ BUT I CAN CORRECT THAT BY...

_____
_____
_____

▶ TODAY'S TOP ACHIEVEMENTS

▶ GYM GOALS
○ _____ ☐
○ _____ ☐
○ _____ ☐

▶ TODAY I'M GRATEFUL FOR...
○ _____
○ _____
○ _____

▶ TODAY I FELT...

(CHOOSE ALL THAT APPLY)

▶ NIGHT PREP FOR TOMORROW
○ _____
○ _____
○ _____

▶ HOW WOULD YOU RATE THE DAY?
☆ ☆ ☆ ☆ ☆

WHAT'S ON YOUR MIND

Use this space to write down **anything** on your mind, that may be influencing you; good, bad or indifferent.

_____

_____

_____

_____

_____

_____

_____

_____

_____

_____

_____

_____

_____

_____

_____

_____

_____

_____

TOMORROW STARTS TODAY

LET'S GO! DATE: _____

▶ **GOALS**
- _____ ☐
- _____ ☐
- _____ ☐
- _____ ☐
- _____ ☐
- _____ ☐
- _____ ☐
- _____ ☐

▶ TODAY I STRUGGLED WITH...

_____
_____
_____
_____

▷ BUT I CAN CORRECT THAT BY...

_____
_____
_____

▶ TODAY'S TOP ACHIEVEMENTS

▶ GYM GOALS
○ _____ ☐
○ _____ ☐
○ _____ ☐

▶ TODAY I'M GRATEFUL FOR...
○ _____
○ _____
○ _____

▶ TODAY I FELT...

(CHOOSE ALL THAT APPLY)

▶ HOW WOULD YOU RATE THE DAY?
☆ ☆ ☆ ☆ ☆

▶ NIGHT PREP FOR TOMORROW
○ _____
○ _____
○ _____

WHAT'S ON YOUR MIND

Use this space to write down **anything** on your mind, that may be influencing you; good, bad or indifferent.

_____

_____

_____

_____

_____

_____

_____

_____

_____

_____

_____

_____

_____

_____

_____

TOMORROW STARTS TODAY

LET'S GO! DATE: _____

▷ GOALS

_____ ☐
_____ ☐
_____ ☐
_____ ☐
_____ ☐
_____ ☐
_____ ☐
_____ ☐

▷ TODAY I STRUGGLED WITH...

_____
_____
_____
_____

▷ BUT I CAN CORRECT THAT BY...

_____
_____
_____

▷ TODAY'S TOP ACHIEVEMENTS

▷ GYM GOALS

○ _____ ☐
○ _____ ☐
○ _____ ☐

▷ TODAY I'M GRATEFUL FOR...

○ _____
○ _____
○ _____

▷ TODAY I FELT...

(CHOOSE ALL THAT APPLY)

▷ NIGHT PREP FOR TOMORROW

○ _____
○ _____
○ _____

▷ HOW WOULD YOU RATE THE DAY?

☆ ☆ ☆ ☆ ☆

WHAT'S ON YOUR MIND

Use this space to write down **anything** on your mind, that may be influencing you;
good, bad or indifferent.

TOMORROW STARTS TODAY

LET'S GO! DATE: _____

▶ GOALS

☐
☐
☐
☐
☐
☐
☐
☐
☐

▶ TODAY I STRUGGLED WITH...

_____
_____
_____
_____

▶ BUT I CAN CORRECT THAT BY...

_____
_____
_____

▶ TODAY'S TOP ACHIEVEMENTS

▶ GYM GOALS
○ _____ ☐
○ _____ ☐
○ _____ ☐

▶ TODAY I'M GRATEFUL FOR...
○ _____
○ _____
○ _____

▶ TODAY I FELT...

(CHOOSE ALL THAT APPLY)

▶ NIGHT PREP FOR TOMORROW
○ _____
○ _____
○ _____

▶ HOW WOULD YOU RATE THE DAY?

☆ ☆ ☆ ☆ ☆

WHAT'S ON YOUR MIND

Use this space to write down **anything** on your mind, that may be influencing you; good, bad or indifferent.

_____

_____

_____

_____

_____

_____

_____

_____

_____

_____

_____

_____

_____

_____

_____

TOMORROW STARTS TODAY

LET'S GO! DATE: _____

▶ **GOALS**
_____ ☐
_____ ☐
_____ ☐
_____ ☐
_____ ☐
_____ ☐
_____ ☐
_____ ☐

▶ TODAY I STRUGGLED WITH...
_____
_____
_____
_____

▶ BUT I CAN CORRECT THAT BY...
_____
_____
_____
_____

▶ TODAY'S TOP ACHIEVEMENTS

▶ GYM GOALS
○ _____ ☐
○ _____ ☐
○ _____ ☐

▶ TODAY I'M GRATEFUL FOR...
○ _____
○ _____
○ _____

▶ TODAY I FELT...
(CHOOSE ALL THAT APPLY)

▶ NIGHT PREP FOR TOMORROW
○ _____
○ _____
○ _____

▶ HOW WOULD YOU RATE THE DAY?
☆ ☆ ☆ ☆ ☆

WHAT'S ON YOUR MIND

Use this space to write down **anything** on your mind, that may be influencing you; good, bad or indifferent.

_____

_____

_____

_____

_____

_____

_____

_____

_____

_____

_____

_____

_____

_____

_____

TOMORROW STARTS TODAY

LET'S GO! DATE: _____

▶ GOALS

- _____ ☐
- _____ ☐
- _____ ☐
- _____ ☐
- _____ ☐
- _____ ☐
- _____ ☐
- _____ ☐
- _____ ☐

▶ TODAY I STRUGGLED WITH...

_____
_____
_____
_____

▶ BUT I CAN CORRECT THAT BY...

_____
_____
_____

▶ TODAY'S TOP ACHIEVEMENTS

▶ GYM GOALS
- ○ _____ ☐
- ○ _____ ☐
- ○ _____ ☐

▶ TODAY I'M GRATEFUL FOR...
- ○ _____
- ○ _____
- ○ _____

▶ TODAY I FELT...

(CHOOSE ALL THAT APPLY)

▶ HOW WOULD YOU RATE THE DAY?

☆ ☆ ☆ ☆ ☆

▶ NIGHT PREP FOR TOMORROW
- ○ _____
- ○ _____
- ○ _____

WHAT'S ON YOUR MIND

Use this space to write down **anything** on your mind, that may be influencing you; good, bad or indifferent.

_____

_____

_____

_____

_____

_____

_____

_____

_____

_____

_____

_____

_____

_____

_____

_____

_____

_____

TOMORROW STARTS TODAY

LET'S GO! DATE: _____

▶ **GOALS**

_____ ☐
_____ ☐
_____ ☐
_____ ☐
_____ ☐
_____ ☐
_____ ☐
_____ ☐

▶ TODAY I STRUGGLED WITH...

_____
_____
_____
_____

▶ TODAY'S TOP ACHIEVEMENTS

▶ TODAY I FELT...

(CHOOSE ALL THAT APPLY)

▶ HOW WOULD YOU RATE THE DAY?

☆ ☆ ☆ ☆ ☆

▶ BUT I CAN CORRECT THAT BY...

_____
_____
_____
_____

▶ GYM GOALS
○ _____ ☐
○ _____ ☐
○ _____ ☐

▶ TODAY I'M GRATEFUL FOR...
○ _____
○ _____
○ _____

▶ NIGHT PREP FOR TOMORROW
○ _____
○ _____
○ _____

WHAT'S ON YOUR MIND

Use this space to write down **anything** on your mind, that may be influencing you;
good, bad or indifferent.

TOMORROW STARTS TODAY

LET'S GO! DATE: _____

▶ **GOALS**

_____ ☐
_____ ☐
_____ ☐
_____ ☐
_____ ☐
_____ ☐
_____ ☐
_____ ☐

▶ TODAY I STRUGGLED WITH...

_____
_____
_____
_____

▶ BUT I CAN CORRECT THAT BY...

_____
_____
_____

▶ TODAY'S TOP ACHIEVEMENTS

▶ GYM GOALS
○ _____ ☐
○ _____ ☐
○ _____ ☐

▶ TODAY I'M GRATEFUL FOR...
○ _____
○ _____
○ _____

▶ TODAY I FELT...

(CHOOSE ALL THAT APPLY)

▶ HOW WOULD YOU RATE THE DAY?
☆ ☆ ☆ ☆ ☆

▶ NIGHT PREP FOR TOMORROW
○ _____
○ _____
○ _____

WHAT'S ON YOUR MIND

Use this space to write down **anything** on your mind, that may be influencing you; good, bad or indifferent.

_____

_____

_____

_____

_____

_____

_____

_____

_____

_____

_____

_____

_____

_____

_____

TOMORROW STARTS TODAY

LET'S GO! DATE: _____

▶ **GOALS**

- _____ ☐
- _____ ☐
- _____ ☐
- _____ ☐
- _____ ☐
- _____ ☐
- _____ ☐
- _____ ☐
- _____ ☐

▶ TODAY I STRUGGLED WITH...

_____
_____
_____
_____

▶ BUT I CAN CORRECT THAT BY...

_____
_____
_____

▶ TODAY'S TOP ACHIEVEMENTS

▶ GYM GOALS
- ○ _____ ☐
- ○ _____ ☐
- ○ _____ ☐

▶ TODAY I'M GRATEFUL FOR...
- ○ _____
- ○ _____
- ○ _____

▶ TODAY I FELT...

(CHOOSE ALL THAT APPLY)

▶ NIGHT PREP FOR TOMORROW
- ○ _____
- ○ _____
- ○ _____

▶ HOW WOULD YOU RATE THE DAY?

☆ ☆ ☆ ☆ ☆

WHAT'S ON YOUR MIND

Use this space to write down **anything** on your mind, that may be influencing you;
good, bad or indifferent.

_____

_____

_____

_____

_____

_____

_____

_____

_____

_____

_____

_____

_____

_____

TOMORROW STARTS TODAY

LET'S GO! DATE: _____

▶ **GOALS**
_____ ☑
_____ ☐
_____ ☐
_____ ☐
_____ ☐
_____ ☐
_____ ☐
_____ ☐
_____ ☐

▶ TODAY I STRUGGLED WITH...
_____
_____
_____
_____

▶ BUT I CAN CORRECT THAT BY...
_____
_____
_____

▶ TODAY'S TOP ACHIEVEMENTS

▶ GYM GOALS
○ _____ ☐
○ _____ ☐
○ _____ ☐

▶ TODAY I'M GRATEFUL FOR...
○ _____
○ _____
○ _____

▶ TODAY I FELT...
😊 😐 😣 😕 😠 🙁
(CHOOSE ALL THAT APPLY)

▶ HOW WOULD YOU RATE THE DAY?
☆ ☆ ☆ ☆ ☆

▶ NIGHT PREP FOR TOMORROW
○ _____
○ _____
○ _____

WHAT'S ON YOUR MIND

Use this space to write down **anything** on your mind, that may be influencing you; good, bad or indifferent.

_____

_____

_____

_____

_____

_____

_____

_____

_____

_____

_____

_____

_____

_____

_____

_____

TOMORROW STARTS TODAY

LET'S GO! DATE: _____

▶ **GOALS**
- _____ ☐
- _____ ☐
- _____ ☐
- _____ ☐
- _____ ☐
- _____ ☐
- _____ ☐
- _____ ☐

▶ TODAY I STRUGGLED WITH...

_____
_____
_____
_____

▶ BUT I CAN CORRECT THAT BY...

_____
_____
_____

▶ TODAY'S TOP ACHIEVEMENTS

▶ GYM GOALS
○ _____ ☐
○ _____ ☐
○ _____ ☐

▶ TODAY I'M GRATEFUL FOR...
○ _____
○ _____
○ _____

▶ TODAY I FELT...

😊 😐 😳 😟 😠 ☹️

(CHOOSE ALL THAT APPLY)

▶ HOW WOULD YOU RATE THE DAY?

☆ ☆ ☆ ☆ ☆

▶ NIGHT PREP FOR TOMORROW
○ _____
○ _____
○ _____

WHAT'S ON YOUR MIND

Use this space to write down **anything** on your mind, that may be influencing you; good, bad or indifferent.

TOMORROW STARTS TODAY

LET'S GO! DATE: _____

▶ **GOALS**
- _____ ☑
- _____ ☐
- _____ ☐
- _____ ☐
- _____ ☐
- _____ ☐
- _____ ☐
- _____ ☐
- _____ ☐

▶ TODAY I STRUGGLED WITH...
_____
_____
_____
_____

▶ BUT I CAN CORRECT THAT BY...
_____
_____
_____

▶ TODAY'S TOP ACHIEVEMENTS

▶ GYM GOALS
- ○ _____ ☐
- ○ _____ ☐
- ○ _____ ☐

▶ TODAY I'M GRATEFUL FOR...
- ○ _____
- ○ _____
- ○ _____

▶ TODAY I FELT...

(CHOOSE ALL THAT APPLY)

▶ HOW WOULD YOU RATE THE DAY?
☆ ☆ ☆ ☆ ☆

▶ NIGHT PREP FOR TOMORROW
- ○ _____
- ○ _____
- ○ _____

WHAT'S ON YOUR MIND

Use this space to write down **anything** on your mind, that may be influencing you; good, bad or indifferent.

TOMORROW STARTS TODAY

LET'S GO! DATE: _____

GOALS

▷ _____ ☐
_____ ☐
_____ ☐
_____ ☐
_____ ☐
_____ ☐
_____ ☐
_____ ☐
_____ ☐

▷ TODAY I STRUGGLED WITH...

_____
_____
_____
_____

▷ TODAY'S TOP ACHIEVEMENTS

▷ TODAY I FELT...

(CHOOSE ALL THAT APPLY)

▷ HOW WOULD YOU RATE THE DAY?
☆ ☆ ☆ ☆ ☆

▷ BUT I CAN CORRECT THAT BY...

_____
_____
_____
_____

▷ GYM GOALS
○ _____ ☐
○ _____ ☐
○ _____ ☐

▷ TODAY I'M GRATEFUL FOR...
○ _____
○ _____
○ _____

▷ NIGHT PREP FOR TOMORROW
○ _____
○ _____
○ _____

WHAT'S ON YOUR MIND

Use this space to write down **anything** on your mind, that may be influencing you; good, bad or indifferent.

TOMORROW STARTS TODAY

LET'S GO! DATE: _____

▶ **GOALS**
- _____ ☐
- _____ ☐
- _____ ☐
- _____ ☐
- _____ ☐
- _____ ☐
- _____ ☐
- _____ ☐

▶ TODAY I STRUGGLED WITH...
_____
_____
_____
_____

▶ BUT I CAN CORRECT THAT BY...
_____
_____
_____

▶ TODAY'S TOP ACHIEVEMENTS

▶ GYM GOALS
○ _____ ☐
○ _____ ☐
○ _____ ☐

▶ TODAY I'M GRATEFUL FOR...
○ _____
○ _____
○ _____

▶ TODAY I FELT...
(CHOOSE ALL THAT APPLY)

▶ NIGHT PREP FOR TOMORROW
○ _____
○ _____
○ _____

▶ HOW WOULD YOU RATE THE DAY?
☆ ☆ ☆ ☆ ☆

WHAT'S ON YOUR MIND

Use this space to write down **anything** on your mind, that may be influencing you; good, bad or indifferent.

_____

_____

_____

_____

_____

_____

_____

_____

_____

_____

_____

_____

_____

_____

_____

TOMORROW STARTS TODAY

LET'S GO! DATE: _____

▶ **GOALS**

_____ ☐
_____ ☐
_____ ☐
_____ ☐
_____ ☐
_____ ☐
_____ ☐
_____ ☐

▶ TODAY I STRUGGLED WITH...

_____
_____
_____
_____

▶ BUT I CAN CORRECT THAT BY...

_____
_____
_____

▶ TODAY'S TOP ACHIEVEMENTS

▶ GYM GOALS

○ _____ ☐
○ _____ ☐
○ _____ ☐

▶ TODAY I'M GRATEFUL FOR...

○ _____
○ _____
○ _____

▶ TODAY I FELT...

(CHOOSE ALL THAT APPLY)

▶ NIGHT PREP FOR TOMORROW

○ _____
○ _____
○ _____

▶ HOW WOULD YOU RATE THE DAY?

☆ ☆ ☆ ☆ ☆

WHAT'S ON YOUR MIND

Use this space to write down **anything** on your mind, that may be influencing you; good, bad or indifferent.

_____

_____

_____

_____

_____

_____

_____

_____

_____

_____

_____

_____

_____

_____

_____

_____

TOMORROW STARTS TODAY

LET'S GO! DATE: _____

▶ GOALS

_____ ☐
_____ ☐
_____ ☐
_____ ☐
_____ ☐
_____ ☐
_____ ☐
_____ ☐

▶ TODAY I STRUGGLED WITH...

_____
_____
_____
_____

▶ BUT I CAN CORRECT THAT BY...

_____
_____
_____

▶ TODAY'S TOP ACHIEVEMENTS

▶ GYM GOALS
○ _____ ☐
○ _____ ☐
○ _____ ☐

▶ TODAY I'M GRATEFUL FOR...
○ _____
○ _____
○ _____

▶ TODAY I FELT...

(CHOOSE ALL THAT APPLY)

▶ NIGHT PREP FOR TOMORROW
○ _____
○ _____
○ _____

▶ HOW WOULD YOU RATE THE DAY?

☆ ☆ ☆ ☆ ☆

WHAT'S ON YOUR MIND

Use this space to write down **anything** on your mind, that may be influencing you; good, bad or indifferent.

_____

_____

_____

_____

_____

_____

_____

_____

_____

_____

_____

_____

_____

_____

TOMORROW STARTS TODAY

LET'S GO! DATE: _____

▶ **GOALS**
- _____ ☐
- _____ ☐
- _____ ☐
- _____ ☐
- _____ ☐
- _____ ☐
- _____ ☐
- _____ ☐
- _____ ☐

▶ TODAY I STRUGGLED WITH...
_____
_____
_____
_____

▶ BUT I CAN CORRECT THAT BY...
_____
_____
_____
_____

▶ TODAY'S TOP ACHIEVEMENTS

▶ GYM GOALS
○ _____ ☐
○ _____ ☐
○ _____ ☐

▶ TODAY I'M GRATEFUL FOR...
○ _____
○ _____
○ _____

▶ TODAY I FELT...
(CHOOSE ALL THAT APPLY)

▶ HOW WOULD YOU RATE THE DAY?
☆ ☆ ☆ ☆ ☆

▶ NIGHT PREP FOR TOMORROW
○ _____
○ _____
○ _____

WHAT'S ON YOUR MIND

Use this space to write down **anything** on your mind, that may be influencing you;
good, bad or indifferent.

_____

_____

_____

_____

_____

_____

_____

_____

_____

_____

_____

_____

_____

TOMORROW STARTS TODAY

LET'S GO! DATE: _____

▶ **GOALS**
- _____ ☑
- _____ ☐
- _____ ☐
- _____ ☐
- _____ ☐
- _____ ☐
- _____ ☐
- _____ ☐

▶ **TODAY I STRUGGLED WITH...**
_____
_____
_____
_____

▶ **BUT I CAN CORRECT THAT BY...**
_____
_____
_____

▶ **TODAY'S TOP ACHIEVEMENTS**

▶ **GYM GOALS**
- ○ _____ ☐
- ○ _____ ☐
- ○ _____ ☐

▶ **TODAY I'M GRATEFUL FOR...**
- ○ _____
- ○ _____
- ○ _____

▶ **TODAY I FELT...**
(CHOOSE ALL THAT APPLY)

▶ **NIGHT PREP FOR TOMORROW**
- ○ _____
- ○ _____
- ○ _____

▶ **HOW WOULD YOU RATE THE DAY?**
☆ ☆ ☆ ☆ ☆

WHAT'S ON YOUR MIND

Use this space to write down **anything** on your mind, that may be influencing you; good, bad or indifferent.

TOMORROW STARTS TODAY

LET'S GO! DATE: _____

▶ **GOALS**
_____ ☐
_____ ☐
_____ ☐
_____ ☐
_____ ☐
_____ ☐
_____ ☐
_____ ☐

▶ TODAY I STRUGGLED WITH...
_____
_____
_____
_____

▶ BUT I CAN CORRECT THAT BY...
_____
_____
_____
_____

▶ TODAY'S TOP ACHIEVEMENTS

▶ GYM GOALS
○ _____ ☐
○ _____ ☐
○ _____ ☐

▶ TODAY I'M GRATEFUL FOR...
○ _____
○ _____
○ _____

▶ TODAY I FELT...

(CHOOSE ALL THAT APPLY)

▶ HOW WOULD YOU RATE THE DAY?
☆ ☆ ☆ ☆ ☆

▶ NIGHT PREP FOR TOMORROW
○ _____
○ _____
○ _____

WHAT'S ON YOUR MIND

Use this space to write down **anything** on your mind, that may be influencing you; good, bad or indifferent.

_____

_____

_____

_____

_____

_____

_____

_____

_____

_____

_____

_____

_____

_____

_____

_____

_____

TOMORROW STARTS TODAY

LET'S GO! DATE: _____

▶ **GOALS**
- _____ ☑
- _____ ☐
- _____ ☐
- _____ ☐
- _____ ☐
- _____ ☐
- _____ ☐
- _____ ☐
- _____ ☐

▶ TODAY I STRUGGLED WITH...
_____
_____
_____
_____

▶ BUT I CAN CORRECT THAT BY...
_____
_____
_____

▶ TODAY'S TOP ACHIEVEMENTS

▶ GYM GOALS
○ _____ ☐
○ _____ ☐
○ _____ ☐

▶ TODAY I'M GRATEFUL FOR...
○ _____
○ _____
○ _____

▶ TODAY I FELT...

(CHOOSE ALL THAT APPLY)

▶ NIGHT PREP FOR TOMORROW
○ _____
○ _____
○ _____

▶ HOW WOULD YOU RATE THE DAY?
☆ ☆ ☆ ☆ ☆

WHAT'S ON YOUR MIND

Use this space to write down **anything** on your mind, that may be influencing you; good, bad or indifferent.

_____

_____

_____

_____

_____

_____

_____

_____

_____

_____

_____

_____

_____

_____

_____

_____

TOMORROW STARTS TODAY

LET'S GO! DATE: _____

▶ **G O A L S**
- _____ ☐
- _____ ☐
- _____ ☐
- _____ ☐
- _____ ☐
- _____ ☐
- _____ ☐
- _____ ☐
- _____ ☐

▶ TODAY I STRUGGLED WITH...

_____
_____
_____
_____

▶ BUT I CAN CORRECT THAT BY...

_____
_____
_____
_____

▶ TODAY'S TOP ACHIEVEMENTS

▶ GYM GOALS
○ _____ ☐
○ _____ ☐
○ _____ ☐

▶ TODAY I'M GRATEFUL FOR...
○ _____
○ _____
○ _____

▶ TODAY I FELT...

(CHOOSE ALL THAT APPLY)

▶ HOW WOULD YOU RATE THE DAY?
☆ ☆ ☆ ☆ ☆

▶ NIGHT PREP FOR TOMORROW
○ _____
○ _____
○ _____

WHAT'S ON YOUR MIND

Use this space to write down **anything** on your mind, that may be influencing you;
good, bad or indifferent.

_____

_____

_____

_____

_____

_____

_____

_____

_____

_____

_____

_____

_____

_____

_____

TOMORROW STARTS TODAY

LET'S GO! DATE: _____

▶ **GOALS**
_____ ☐
_____ ☐
_____ ☐
_____ ☐
_____ ☐
_____ ☐
_____ ☐
_____ ☐

▶ TODAY I STRUGGLED WITH...
_____
_____
_____
_____

▶ BUT I CAN CORRECT THAT BY...
_____
_____
_____

▶ TODAY'S TOP ACHIEVEMENTS

▶ GYM GOALS
○ _____ ☐
○ _____ ☐
○ _____ ☐

▶ TODAY I'M GRATEFUL FOR...
○ _____
○ _____
○ _____

▶ TODAY I FELT...

(CHOOSE ALL THAT APPLY)

▶ HOW WOULD YOU RATE THE DAY?
☆ ☆ ☆ ☆ ☆

▶ NIGHT PREP FOR TOMORROW
○ _____
○ _____
○ _____

WHAT'S ON YOUR MIND

Use this space to write down **anything** on your mind, that may be influencing you;
good, bad or indifferent.

TOMORROW STARTS TODAY

LET'S GO! DATE: _____

▶ **GOALS**

- _____ ☑
- _____ ☐
- _____ ☐
- _____ ☐
- _____ ☐
- _____ ☐
- _____ ☐
- _____ ☐
- _____ ☐

▶ TODAY I STRUGGLED WITH...

_____
_____
_____
_____

▶ BUT I CAN CORRECT THAT BY...

_____
_____
_____
_____

▶ TODAY'S TOP ACHIEVEMENTS

▶ GYM GOALS
○ _____ ☐
○ _____ ☐
○ _____ ☐

▶ TODAY I'M GRATEFUL FOR...
○ _____
○ _____
○ _____

▶ TODAY I FELT...

(CHOOSE ALL THAT APPLY)

▶ HOW WOULD YOU RATE THE DAY?
☆ ☆ ☆ ☆ ☆

▶ NIGHT PREP FOR TOMORROW
○ _____
○ _____
○ _____

WHAT'S ON YOUR MIND

Use this space to write down **anything** on your mind, that may be influencing you; good, bad or indifferent.

_____

_____

_____

_____

_____

_____

_____

_____

_____

_____

_____

_____

_____

_____

_____

TOMORROW STARTS TODAY

LET'S GO! DATE: _____

▶ **GOALS**

_____ ☐
_____ ☐
_____ ☐
_____ ☐
_____ ☐
_____ ☐
_____ ☐
_____ ☐
_____ ☐

▶ TODAY I STRUGGLED WITH...

_____
_____
_____
_____

▶ BUT I CAN CORRECT THAT BY...

_____
_____
_____

▶ TODAY'S TOP ACHIEVEMENTS

▶ GYM GOALS
○ _____ ☐
○ _____ ☐
○ _____ ☐

▶ TODAY I'M GRATEFUL FOR...
○ _____
○ _____
○ _____

▶ TODAY I FELT...

(CHOOSE ALL THAT APPLY)

▶ HOW WOULD YOU RATE THE DAY?

☆ ☆ ☆ ☆ ☆

▶ NIGHT PREP FOR TOMORROW
○ _____
○ _____
○ _____

WHAT'S ON YOUR MIND

Use this space to write down **anything** on your mind, that may be influencing you;
good, bad or indifferent.

_____

_____

_____

_____

_____

_____

_____

_____

_____

_____

_____

_____

_____

_____

TOMORROW STARTS TODAY

Made in the USA
Las Vegas, NV
14 November 2023

80861202R00070